Annette Kaiser
99 Questions to a
Spiritual Teacher

Annette Kaiser
99 Questions to a Spiritual Teacher

Published by Eos

ISBN 978-0-9892289-7-8

Printed and Bound in the United States

EOS

Contents

For You

Questions about
Spirituality

1.   What is spirituality for you?

In quintessence, spirituality for me is wakeful, joyful Being-Presence from moment to moment. And within this vibrates the boundless feeling of deep and unconditional love for everything and all at once – clear as a diamond.

This spirituality unifies Being and Becoming and expresses itself in a way of living as a world citizen, locally and globally, here and now.

When did you first come into contact with spirituality? Could you describe this experience?

In essence it is the result of a long, inner journey.

At the age of 14, I spent time in a monastery in Paris, where I was learning French and working at the same time. It was there that a first spiritual contact occurred. I went to church – it may have been around the evening service – and heard the novices singing, luminously bright, clear like the stars in the sky and pure. It went right through me and stirred me deeply. It was as if I had tasted the core of That without a name – an irreversible touch. Here began the pathless path into Nothingness – all that is. It is the greatest adventure ever.

2.   Is a person walking a spiritual path a better person?

Whether a person is better than another can be recognized by the traces they leave behind. People who are walking a spiritual path become more conscious and sensitive, and are likely more aware when they hurt other beings.

For such people, it is easier to forgive – themselves and others. That is why they leave fewer traces – on other human beings and on this planet.

They act for the Greater Good, for everything and all that is. And that is noticeable. Whether or not a person calls themselves spiritual is not the point. Rather, it is about the way in which we humans love, unconditionally, as the One Heart.

How do you see the relation between a student's effort and grace on the spiritual path?

Effort and grace are not really comparable. They are words that describe meaning on two different levels: Effort arises where there is resistance. This can be both gross and subtle. Grace is not causal. She cannot really be described, although she is inherent in everything that is.

Here an example:

One day we decide to start practicing yoga or meditation every morning. By doing so, something new is set into motion. On a practical level this means, for example, getting up half an hour earlier every day. That can cause resistance – the body does not want to get out of bed half an hour earlier. So initially some effort is required, a form of discipline.

But quite soon we will notice, perhaps with surprise, that meditating in the morning has become a gift.

We observe that our regular morning practice gives us a peaceful strength that stays with us throughout the day. Getting up in the morning becomes effortless - our inertia is overcome.

Maybe the experience of this peaceful strength can be called grace. Grace is ever-present, always and everywhere. Perhaps we simply had not noticed her until now.

Everything – every form and shape– is full of grace.

Do you believe that being a spiritual teacher is a special act of grace?

How can I answer this question!

A spiritual teacher has no face and no name. In pure Being everything is pure grace. It is utterly impersonal. At the same time, there is also a person with talents, strengths, and weaknesses – a continuous becoming.

From this perspective, I feel like a fish in the water as a spiritual teacher – in complete harmony with body, mind, and soul.

This may best be described as vocation. When one experiences vocation in everything one is doing, the forces of the soul start guiding the life of a human being.

4. Can enlightenment be attained through effort?

The first question should be: What is enlightenment? It has to do with light, with the light that is Consciousness Itself. This light, which is inherent in all and yet transcends all, still remains mostly hidden to us humans. We cannot see this light with our eyes, nor can we grasp it with our minds. But IT IS. Brighter than a thousand suns, it shines in the Heart of Hearts.

The question of whether one can attain enlightenment through effort cannot be answered as such.

We can all notice that as people get older, they do not automatically become wiser and more compassionate for everything that is.

At the same time, there is no effort that can lead to enlightenment. How could it! Enlightenment – light – has always been and always will be, beyond our existence. As soon as a person ceases to hold their identification with "I" and "mine" as a separate being, the light will reveal itself as pure Consciousness in Being and Becoming.

5. How do you think will people's engagement with spirituality change in the future?

In the near future, spiritual paths will condense towards the essence of all spiritual paths. In the distant future, what we allege to be spiritual paths may even become redundant.

Consciousness is conscious.

Recognizing this is the next evolutionary step in human development.

It is a quiet (r)evolution – self-emanating Reality IS Consciousness – self-revealing, self-organizing, ego-transcending, inseparable Oneness in Being and Becoming.

One day it will be completely natural for humanity to see the power of presence within the indivisible Unity of all Being and Becoming, in all its diversity, as the foundation of life.

What exactly makes you so sure about this?

The perspective of evolution gives me a sense of it. First of all, the human species is still very young on this planet. It has the potential to develop further.

Today we know that evolution has a direction: It moves towards complexity and greater depths of consciousness. At this point in time, humanity has not yet fully unfolded its gift of being conscious. What is required is total presence from moment to moment, of thinking, feeling, acting... conscious Being. It is not until then that we can speak of being truly human.

This is the potential that lies within the human species. Whether or not humanity will make use of this is another question.

6. What message in the spiritual domain is most important for you today?

Today I understand that every moment is an invitation into Reality Itself. It transcends body, mind, emotions, the world itself – all forms that come and go – and yet contains all that is at once.

This is an incredible opportunity for humanity. It is a quiet (r)evolution, which has the potential of leaving behind a separating worldview. Thereby, it is the basis for a new civilization.

That, for me, is the most important message.

7. Can the spiritual ever be a replacement for the secular?

The spiritual and the secular are inseparably One. In my understanding there is only One Reality – That without a name. Arising in it is the world with all forms that come and go. All is inseparably the One Reality.

Reality Itself is acausal, while its various modifications are based on causality. Spirituality can bring us closer to the One Reality, through which the perspective of the world and self fundamentally changes. This is known as the Great Liberation: Normal at last!

What moment or process was it, in which you realized or experience this for yourself?

A deep insight was granted to me in India. I was meditating, and suddenly there was no body anymore, only the limitless sky and beyond that pure Emptiness… nothing but the Nothingness, nobody experiencing anything.

Later I got up and started walking along the ocean, and I saw myself in everything that is: I was the fleas in the fur of a stray dog, the ocean, the sky, the sand and its every grain, the drifting clouds, every single breath of everything that is and is not…and everything all at once. It was the beginning of understanding that which is Reality.

8. Spirituality often appears to be very deep and serious – how important is humor for you in spiritual work?

Humor is very important when engaging a spiritual practice. Mrs.Tweedie once told us that a spiritual path without humor is not a real spiritual path. It is especially good to be able to laugh about yourself, to not take yourself too seriously and to be able to meet the small and big things in life with a big heart-smile. It means being less identified with oneself, and that makes room for your soul – for yourself as well as for others.

When Reality is recognized as that which IS, you might just start laughing. In fact, you might laugh so hard that you cry, as the belief that one is a separate being is the greatest cosmic joke!

Why, in your understanding, do many great religions still convey their content with exactly this seriousness – often working on the basis of intrinsic guilt and badness of the person?

Truthfulness and sincerity are essential on the spiritual journey. And it is especially these two qualities that entail the real humor, when everything falls away into Nothingness.

In addition, simply being human has something humorous about it. I am thinking here of the wonderful story of Nasrudin. He is known as a story teller, a kind of fool, who recognizes humanness in all its different shades and propensities. We laugh about these stories because something within us understands clearly: There are aspects within us that just seem really funny when observed from a distance. That religion conveys sincerity makes sense. It calls upon the fundamentals, to that, which is the essence of life, divinity and humanness. Interestingly, you did not mention truthfulness in your question. Over time, many religions have developed into institutions with particular interests. Originally, all religions were intrinsically committed to sincerity and truthfulness. With the institutionalization, a mixed field developed, which, amongst original interests (religio – to go to the root) started representing particular interests of power and control.

Questions of guilt are related to this. The badness of the human being contains a judgment, and judgment is based on separation.

There is no good or bad person per se. That is a dual understanding of the nature of things. Life itself is fundamentally friendly. A goodness underlies Reality that is beyond good and bad.

9.   What is a Sufi?

From a traditional perspective, one would say as Sufi is one whose heart is as soft and warm as wool. Another answer is this: A Sufi is no one. Both of these descriptions point to the essence of what it means to be human: Being-love that is All, and holds everything and all that is in its deep compassion, and which also recognizes the transparency of all form – emptiness.

Why did you choose the path of a Sufi as a young woman? Is it even right to speak about this as a choice?

Essential for me was the radical nature of this path – radical in the sense of "going back to the root". When I read Irina Tweedie's book "Daughter of Fire: A Diary of a Spiritual Training with a Sufi

Master" in 1982, I knew that it was about, "to be or not to be" – that is, to die and to be. Being fully engaged in life offered me an opportunity for deep self-realization.

Back then I had two young children, worked part-time and had a deep desire to commit my life to the One. The path of love, as Mrs. Tweedie had walked it, was a guiding light for this deep longing. For three years, I simply observed Mrs. Tweedie, as I did not understand what was happening here. Something at the root of my being was fascinated. I knew I had finally arrived. The fact that Mrs. Tweedie was embodying the path of a Sufi was somehow secondary. Love was the centre point of this path and that was universal for me.

I understand religion as something that leads back to the root, to Truth Itself, beyond any religious interpretation.

10. Spirituality and politics – how do you perceive the relationship between the two?

Spirituality conveys the essence of the essence to us human beings, within which Being and Becoming are inseparably One. In its original sense, politics is a sort of tool that is meant to maintain the cosmically prevailing laws in a society.

However, politics has long ceased to represent this original function. It is rather influenced by a mixed field of consciousness: By good intentions on the one hand, but also by financial dependencies and the securing of vested interests on the other.

That is why Bhai Sahib (teacher of Irina Tweedie) had warned about mixing spiritual and political matters. Looking at the 20th Century, the reason for this becomes very obvious. For example, it is known that Adolf Hitler was not averse to pseudomystical and pseudospiritual approaches. An incredible abuse! The collective – and particularly the unconscious collective – is unpredictable and manipulable in this respect.

At the same time there have always been Sufis, as Mrs. Tweedie, who are active in politics, education, culture or economics, in order to contribute in the spirit of the One.

Today, I believe, a different era is dawning. More and more, we have the possibility to recognize clearly what is. That is, we have the gift of discernment in order to see which dimension of consciousness is thought, spoken and acted through. We understand the language of the heart more and more, which is always dedicated to the welfare of the inseparable Whole.

And of course, a spiritual, conscious person is awake:

They understand what is happening in his environment, what is happening in the world, as they are a part of everything and are everything at once.

I believe that today, spirituality should also express itself naturally in political engagement. This means that we stand for the One World, for a new culture, which serves the good of all. We stand for a life in dignity for all living beings on the basis of the always existing Unity. Political approaches along these lines already exist: For example, in Switzerland there is the Integrale Partei and in Germany the Violette Partei.

At the same time, it is important that every single person stands and acts upon a freely chosen responsibility for everyone and all, locally and globally. That we also start talking publicly about the inseparable Unity of all life, which reveals the different layers of existence, in order to grow out of the matrix of fear and into the matrix of love and wisdom. The problems we face today can only be resolved from the recognition that everything and all IS everybody all at once.

11. What is the difference between spirituality and esotericism for you?

The word esoteric means secret knowledge. Secret teachings and knowledge were only shared with selected people. It was knowledge that was kept hidden away from the general public – probably for many different reasons.

The exoteric teachings were intended for a more general audience and thus presented in more common, readily comprehensible language. Esoteric paths were, until the Forties of the last century, mostly secret paths, to which only few human beings had access.

I can clearly remember the Dalai Lama saying in the presence of the

Hopi-eldest – I believe it was in the Seventies – that from now on, spiritual teachings and paths would be open to all people. The time had come for the inner or secret teachings to become accessible to all of humanity.

Esotericism is a big and booming market. Books, CD's, clothing, incense, many different courses and self-declared gurus and healers. People seeking meaning spend more money than ever on these things. What do you think about this?

Whatever helps people to become more conscious and to awaken, I support. A certain book, a prayer, or a scent that touches eternity can be an inspiration for this.

However, already in the Fifties, Bhai Sahib talked about a time to come in which a guru or healer will jump up from underneath every stone that is overturned. What is needed here is the gift of discrimination.

When all this becomes commerce as you said, it will gradually lose its light quality.

It is light, which creates.

12. I have the impression that spirituality is becoming more and more appealing to those who used to view spirituality with skepticism. I am talking, for example, about people in management and leadership positions. What are you views on this trend and where do you think it is heading?

In principal, this is a very welcome development and one that fills me with great joy. And yet of course, the spiritual dimension can, as has happened so often, be abused for personal interests. A mindfulness training, which is being conducted in an organization, can indeed lead to more relaxed and concentrated employees and therefore contribute to less stress and more joy at the workplace. That is wonderful and there is no abuse in this. Abuse occurs where there is the intention to maximize only one specific part, which prevents an optimization of the whole on a global scale.

Real spirituality goes much further: It inquires within the depths of the context of everybody and all at once. It asks whether the organization, for example, contributes to the greater good, whether resources are carefully used, whether the product serves all of humanity, and so on. Indeed, it reveals an entirely new perspective that is rooted being all One. Within this, a new intelligence becomes accessible, which allows cooperation, globally and locally, and tolerance to express itself creatively in thought, word and action.

This does not mean that it is necessary to shut down an organization, but rather calls for a new orientation and intention, which serves the good of all: The employees as well as the entrepreneurs, within the context of the One World.

Do you intentionally seek out such people or do you let them find you? How important is it to you to be in dialogue and exchange with leaders in economics and politics?

I always follow the inner light. If there is the clear impulse to approach someone, I do so.

Otherwise, I am. That means that I meet the right people at the right time at the right place. There are no important or unimportant people for me. Besides, I do not believe that today's leaders in economics and politics alone have the power to transform our current global system. That will only be possible for a predominantly conscious humanity.

13. When is a person enlightened? And does the "attained" enlightenment stably persist?

A persTon is never enlightened. As only when the seemingly separated I merges in the Great I of all Being and non-Being, IT shines.
Reality is light.
In Presence, light is clear and unbounded. Consciousness manifests in love.

Presence is awareness. In being present, there is neither a subject nor an object – Consciousness is conscious, from moment to moment, always new. For us human beings, this is a radically new dimension of consciousness. The caterpillar is the butterfly.

In observing our mind and thoughts, we can first trace this One Taste between each thought or between every breath.

A true first experience of Presence, however, is always an act of grace – often only a brief insight. After that, the task is to identify everything that clouds or obscures this taste and to let go of the associated identifications.

Eckart Tolle speaks about three fundamental aspects that can cloud Presence or awareness: attachment, resistance and judgment.

The essence of the present moment always radiates in light. As soon as we reject something that is present now, or desperately want something, we lose presence. To be awake in the Here and Now requires life-long cultivation. Yet, over time, presence becomes increasingly easy. Conditioning becomes noticeable as movement, without the radiance of the light being affected. The intensity of presence increases in depth.

In true Awareness, though, there is neither time nor particular depth. It Is.

14. What is awakening? How do enlightenment and awakening relate?

Awakening may describe more of a process involved in transforming the ego identity, while the word enlightenment emphasizes the light-shift. To awaken means not to sleep or dream anymore. The illusion of being an independent, separate being means to be asleep.

Awakening means total self-recognition. Reality is inseparably One, self-radiant, self-revealing, and within this arises the causal world of forms and their evolutionary development.

Can you say something about shadow work? How can one work with one's

shadow? What is the relationship between enlightenment and shadow?
Awakening means that you are automatically confronted with your own shadow. This is because ignorance and unilluminated living are related to one's shadows.

As we grow up, we are subject to personal, familial and societal conditioning. For example, parents may have particular ideas about which characteristics their child should have, as for example "not being too loud". The child soon learns that it is rewarded in its family for being quiet. One way it might respond to this is by suppressing its natural loudness, in order to be loved. Later, as an adult, this person may react to any loudness with an outburst of anger…

This calls for the resolution of the shadow complex in the light of awareness, in order to transform the reactive mechanisms. With a bit of practice, the shadow work will get easier and easier and perhaps will even become a friend.

This gives me the opportunity to recognize myself on a deeper and deeper level, and to cultivate compassion for everyone involved. This is how we grow into a mature human being. The mirror of the heart becomes increasingly clear; the transformation of the heart, the change in consciousness takes place: The human being is awakens.

15. How does the awareness of a conscious person differ to that of an unconscious person?

Indeed, there is a fundamental difference. The one who is deluded, or not conscious, experiences themselves as a separate being, separated from all other people, separated from the world, as well as separated from THAT, which is beyond the unnameable.

Last year I was in Cambodia to support a school project, which especially focuses on enabling girls to have a school education.

In Cambodia there is the virgin trade. That means that girls from about 12 years of age are sold as virgins for little money. For the poor population this is a common way to earn money. That is an extremely brutal thing.

Inner strength, serenity and boundless love are required in order to really look closely at this. The suffering in Cambodia, which in part can still be traced back to the era of Pol Pot, is unbearable. So here I was, intensively practicing being able to face this human horror without being overcome by the suffering, nor developing a general feeling of rejection towards the perpetrators, in a deep understanding that there is no separation.

Out of this perspective, an intensity of loving kindness arises. And within it, one simply does what is required.

It is a very natural, spontaneous action, which emanates out of being present here and now. I am neither doing something good, nor do I want to eradicate anything. Love in action has the power to transcend.

Because of my many years in development work in the 3rd world, I know the difference very well; development work assumes a fundamental separation between self and world. Even with the intention to do the very best thing possible, which is an honorable intention, new complications occur instead of real development.

The level of consciousness of a development expert is therefore crucial and lays out a guiding thread of light.

From a place of Unity, it is not about a desire to help or to behave in a politically correct way and so on. In the present, wakeful Being, everything and all is inseparably One. Inherent in it is a form of love – some call it compassion or agape, which wishes to act from and out of itself, for the well-being of all creatures, wherever one may be at any given time.

This gives everything a totally different foundation. I do not expect gratitude, I do not give and the other person does not receive. All of this disappears. Giving and taking are a single flow of life.

Through this, dependencies, entanglements, resistances, attachments etc. – all aspects of the "I" and "mine" do not develop. People feel this instantly. It becomes an encounter from heart to heart.

16. Are there also people who will not reach enlightenment despite long, spiritual practice? And if so, why do you think that is?

In traditional understanding this was the case. Not all spiritual people, even those with a serious practice, were graced to have a breakthrough into Reality. Yet, every time a seed was planted that one day would blossom. Nothing is in vain, as every thought, every word, every act itself has an effect. Every intention of a person contributes.

Today, a fundamental change has occurred. Only since the Seventies, spirituality has become accessible to a wide audience. Spiritual teachings used to be kept in secret, only accessible to few selected devotees or certain circles, etc. The fact that this has changed reflects the zeitgeist of evolution: The next evolutionary development will occur through a shift in consciousness. More and more people are able to differentiate between thinking and consciousness, that is, Presence.

The entire consciousness-level of humanity is evolving, so that it is becoming easier for more and more people to get a first taste of Presence. This, however, is only the beginning of a spiritual path.

Today, it is not so much about experiencing the taste of Oneness anymore. It is more about its stabilization, and out of this, developing an integrated way of life. These are the challenges we are facing today, in which Being and Becoming are recognized and lived as inseparably One.

17.   What are your thoughts about karma?

As long as we live in duality, which means defining ourselves as a separate person, we produce traces, or karma. That means that we are residing in a space of cause and effect. Whether we call it karma or not is secondary. As long as we live from the identified I, the law of cause and effect applies: Everything I am thinking, speaking or doing as a separate self produces a polarizing effect.

In pure Presence, in which there is no time, no "I" or "mine", no karmic traces can be produced. That is only possible within time, where subject and object are separated. Presence is acausal. In wakeful Being-Presence from moment to moment it is possible to instantly transform the causally determined dimension. This means that the effective power of cause and effect diminishes – it becomes transparent. Thereby, no new karma emerges, which means that no new patterns of causality develop.

I believe that only very few people are able to sustain pure Presence all the time. Presence is not simply presence. With precise observation we can detect that the power of light, the intensity of Presence, is dynamic. Often, we may be able to detect a mixed field, in which the light of Presence is there, but only briefly – not for long. We also may notice that elements of conditioning enter into this field of Presence; patterns of reaction, which are causally determined.

If, for example, I am being blamed for doing something that I did not do, a reactive pattern is activated in me that wants to immediately defend itself. We all know this. In pure wakeful Presence this automatic reaction pattern can be detected before it is acted upon, and can immediately be transformed in the light of Awareness. If our Presence is even more deeply rooted, patterns of reactivity will not even occur at all.

And so we relax into this wakeful Being and cultivate Presence.

If we lose it, we simply "get back up again", as every moment is an invitation into wakeful Beingness.

The topic of karma is by no means exhausted by this description. Bhai Sahib once said to Mrs. Tweedie that karma is a highly complex issue. What I know with great certainty is that the so-called traces, which we created during our lives, do not simply disappear when we die. The causally determined traces remain as information on a certain level of consciousness, no matter if positively or negatively charged, and continue to have their effects.

Simultaneously, a new era seems to be emerging in the 21st century. Karmic information will lose its effective power in the course of expanding consciousness – not only through us human beings, but seen within a cosmic context.

As soon as we human beings are more and more rooted in the Here and Now, other rules hold.

Isn't that wonderful!

18. Is everyone the creator of their own fortune?

What is fortune? What is misfortune?

Fortune or misfortune
A parable from China:
A farmer was living at the edge of his village and had a field that was just big enough for the farmer to grow everything on it that he needed to live. His wife had died early, and he had raised his own son alone. In the course of his life, the farmer had learnt to accept things in life as they occurred, and so he walked the deep valleys of his life without complaining. Through this, a great ease and deep peacefulness developed inside him. The people of the village appreciated him a lot – they often asked for his advice when the worries of life and the hardship of work seemed overwhelming. And never did anyone leave him, without feeling having they had gained new hope and confidence.

Despite his poverty, the farmer owned a great treasure. This treasure was a horse as white as the snow, and of delicate beauty. And every morning, before beginning his work on the field, he went out to his horse, and spoke with it. He loved his horse a lot, and so every day began in joy for him.

One day, as the framer awoke, he felt a strange emptiness inside him. As he stepped outside, he saw that his white horse had disappeared. As the people of the village head about this, they came to comfort the farmer, as he had always done for them. "Poor famer, what misfortune has hit you! Can there be a worse misfortune that losing everything that one has owned?"

But the farmer stood in front of his cottage, lifted his hand asking for silence and spoke: "How can you speak of misfortune? We only know that my horse has disappeared. Whether this is fortune or misfortune, we do not know."

And indeed, the white horse soon came back, and with it, a herd of forty wild horses. According to the law of the country, these horses now belonged to the farmer, and he became a rich man. This news spread like fire in the entire village. "Quickly, let us go and see the lucky farmer!" exclaimed the people of the village. They were laughing and happy for him, as they ran down the dusty roads towards his cottage. He could hear their happy voices from afar. "Our farmer, he is so fortunate! He was right! Oh, what an intelligent man he is, and so wise! Now he is rich, so rich!" They were deeply happy for him. But strangely, he stood silently in front of his door.

Then he again lifted his hand and as the people of the village became silent, he said: "How can you speak of fortune? All that we know is that my horse came back, and with it forty wild horses that now belong to me. Whether this is fortune or misfortune, we do not know."

The people of the village wondered about this peculiar person, and could not understand him. Many laughed about him. The son of the farmer was now training the horses, one after the other. One day, however, he fell from a horse and broke both of his legs. The farmer has been proved right. "Oh, how wise our farmer is!", the people of the village whispered. They went to tell him this, but he simply responded:

Did you not understand any of what I told you? All we know is that my son fell from a horse and broke both of his legs. Whether this is fortune or misfortune, we do not know."

Shorty after this, a war started, and all able men were called to fight. Only the farmer's son stayed at home. Whether this was a fortune or a misfortune, cannot be said until today.

What we call external fortune is relative within the greater context. And yet, we human beings need a foundation from which a life in dignity is possible. That much "fortune" should be possible for everyone. In this lies the responsibility of every world citizen – to contribute, enable and maintain a foundation of life for every human being to live in dignity. Besides that, it is largely up to us whether we perceive ourselves as fortunate or unfortunate.

Already the Upanishads are telling us that we ourselves are creating the world. And we are probably doing this more than we can imagine in this moment. Reality Itself is inherent love-bliss. That means that in Being-Present, pure joy can be experienced, unconditionally… IT IS – conscious, blissful, empty. This kind of fortune is available to us in every moment.

We realize that life is kind and that every moment dances in the joy of Beingness. This new way of seeing, which is seeing in not-seeing, is real seeing. It puts everything that is perceived into a different light; in this, the experience of drinking a glass of water can be pure bliss or happiness – just like that! It goes without saying that through this "understanding" an entirely different world arises.

19.   There are many religions that have the idea – especially in Christianity – that those who lead a very simple and ascetic life, and may even suffer hardship in one way or another, are closest to God. Are you also of that opinion?

Let us first focus on simple life. Simple in German means "einfach". From a deeper perspective, that means onefold. Living in simplicity (so in ONEness) is of high quality. As world citizens we can think about creating a way of life that allows all people to live in dignity and joy. This is likely to be a way of life in simplicity; simple means here that we only take what we really need in order to live an empowered life in beauty, while holding the entire world, all humans, animals, and plants in our hearts.

This includes the application of intelligent technologies, as well as all knowledge and wisdom of the entire human history that is available to us today. I do not believe in moving backwards, but in an intelligent combination of old and new knowledge that is in harmony with the entire cosmic system. That is a life in simplicity for me.

The ascetic life is something different. Asceticism was the path of many mystic traditions. It was meant to lead to freedom from the bonds, attachment, and the enslavement of this world, which is always associated with the identification with matter. Asceticism did not only enable the realization of the transient nature of everything, but also a disidentifcation from it, allowing eternity to fully shine in the Here and Now. We can see now, however, that in many mystic traditions this lead to a devaluation of matter altogether.

So the ascetic perspectives can clearly lead to a subtle or even gross rejection of matter. This is still noticeable in some spiritual traditions today. The One Reality is inseparably one. Spirit cannot be separated from matter and vice versa, whilst simultaneously they are also not identical.

Mrs. Tweedie said to us that a very poor person, who is barely surviving, often has to struggle more to dedicate themselves to spirituality. She also said that great riches are often obstructive on the spiritual path. The very best way, she said, is being in the middle – not too rich and not too poor. As we in the Western World belong more to the rich, it can be difficult for us to really let go of all identification. There are so many opportunities for us to get caught up in materialism that the true essence can easily get lost.

It is a high art of living to be neither hooked to an ascetic concept, nor to decline to spiritual flatland. Ultimately, it is still about "die and be" This requires great sincerity and truthfulness. But it does not need to be difficult. This, also, is an old concept. It Is.

Does a spiritual teacher also have limits in their compassion?

I believe that in pure Presence, which inherently carries boundless love for everything, there are no limits. This does not mean, however, that I, as a single being, am responsible for everyone and everything. In following the inner light, I pray or speak with people in need, or remain silent and act, if something can be done.

No, compassion is without limits.

If ever I do not experience empathy for a person or in a situation, I inquire within myself and find a yet unidentified shadow aspect within me.

I then illuminate it in consciousness. Once the shadow is completely integrated, I immediately feel deep compassion for its cause.

For me, the question is much more about how I can contribute to reduce suffering in this world. How can compassion be deepened and extended? That is the question that I carry within me.

20. Is it alright for a spiritual person to fully enjoy the pleasures of life?

Yes – when it is done within the context of the whole and does not get caught up in habits. Spirituality also means celebrating the richness of life in simplicity.

Everything is holy. Enjoyment is more about quality than quantity. Most people are not even able to truly enjoy.

It is a real art to fully enjoy an apple – to be fully present with the experience of eating a whole apple. Most of the time we take a half-conscious bite, enjoy the fresh and juicy flavor for a little moment, and then our mind starts wandering off; eating the apple just somehow happens. That means that we are not fully enjoying what Is now. In the here and now the true nature of an apple can be recognized.

In the deepest depths, the entire Universe reveals itself in it.

In my understanding, when one walks a spiritual path, one develops a stronger sensitivity for the whole, the world. Does it not become increasingly impossible to celebrate one's own life and joy in the light of the incredible hardship that so many people experience? How do you do this?

Yes, I understand your question very well.

It is like this: In a way, the entire world is eating this above mentioned apple. If I do this half-heartedly, it does not really serve the world much. If, however, I reside in the light of Awareness, which is inseparably One, light enters this world.

That is what I understand as fully enjoying the pleasures of life.

So the way in which we do things is a matter of quality.

Simultaneously, I do not only eat the apple or go for walks,…

Most of my time is dedicated to people, in service of the whole. But for me this also means fully enjoying life.

While I do this, my soul incessantly sings in the silence.

21. How can I decipher which parts inside me arise from "divine will", and where, instead, my ego is speaking?

That is an important question. In most religions, the conscience of people comes into play in one way or the other. I used to be Catholic, and in this religion, conscience definitely played a large role. It is important to differentiate between conditioned conscience and actual conscience. The conditioned conscience is based on external rules, that is, on do's and don'ts .Actual conscience carries a knowledge within itself that is inherent to all human beings. Conscience – con-science – that means "together knowing", or "joint knowledge" in French and in English.

Conscience is a sort of inner entity, which clearly knows what contributes to the greater good. If we turn deeply inward and ask ourselves what should and should not be done, we receive an answer – as far as we are really interested in an answer that lies beyond personal preferences or aversions.

This inner entity becomes increasingly clearer with practice. More and more, we perceive it as our inner voice. It has a distinct flavor that sets it apart from all other inner voices; it is without question, to the point and crystal clear. Something in us knows.

It requires good observation skills and also some time to learn to differentiate the different voices within ourselves. When the "I" is speaking that really wants or does not want something for itself, this also has a particular flavor. I would describe it as sharp, demanding and coarse. And then there are also many mixed fields, which are a concoction of vital, emotional and mental elements. With clear observation, these mixed fields become increasingly noticeable. When we are deeply rooted in Presence, the inner voice of our actual conscience ceases to be a voice, a separate thing, and becomes part of the Being-flow that is available to us in every moment.

Questions about the
Teacher-Student Relationship

22.   When is it good to seek a spiritual teacher?

Seeking a spiritual teacher can be good when there is an inner calling to do so, or when someone has touched you spiritually in a deep way. Traditionally we say that the teacher finds the student. Further, it can be helpful to step into contact with a spiritual teacher if one has had spiritual experiences that are difficult to understand or to integrate. It can also simply be helpful to be accompanied by a spiritual friend on one's path to becoming fully human.

It is not unusual to hear about abuse in the teacher-student relationship. Can you say something about this?

Abuse in a teacher-student relationship is and will continue to be an issue. Bhai Sahib therefore called everyone to thoroughly assess a potential teacher. Money, sex, possession and power over people are all factors that play a role in the gross realm. But more subtle forms of abuse are also possible, for example through the development of dependencies. The teacher-student relationship is a very sensitive field. If a person is hurt or deluded in it, this can result in deep trauma.

Mrs. Tweedie said to us that the Sufi path is a path for adults.

That means that students also need to be responsible for themselves. We do not follow a teacher blindly. Everything a teacher says is received with an awake and open heart and assessed in one's own heart. Only after this, action follows.

We have extensively discussed and written about the teacher-student relationship in the integral movement. It is good to be informed!

If an abuse by one's own teacher is identified, I would first seek to speak with the teacher, and if this is not met with resonance, I would raise this issue in the sangha.

65

HOTEL BÄREN
INTERLAKEN · WILDERSWIL

Ihre Rechnung

Tisch 57

| 1 Menusalat | 1 | 6.00 |
| 1 Winzer Rösti | 1 | 18.00 |

SUMME 24.00

Hotel *(signature)* 24.00

CHE-109.871.208 MWST
| 1 7.70% | 1.72 | 22.28 | 24.00 |

Es bediente Sie Vladimir

www.baeren.ch / 033 827 02 02

Montag 16. Jul 2018 20:45
Kassenstelle 01 Coupon 029'103
Service 03

23. How does the teacher recognize the student and the student the teacher?

This differs from person to person. There are no rules. What is sure is that it is an intimate heart-matter – not necessarily outwardly obvious, but noticeable on the deepest Being-level. There is light-resonance. Sometimes this may only slowly enter consciousness. But there is always something for the student, which touches and activates Silence.

For the teacher it is different. The teacher does not seek students, but IS.

When someone approaches the teacher with the heart-wish to receive spiritual guidance, they merely assess whether this wish is truthful. If this is the case, they welcome every student.

Are there students that you have distanced yourself from – internally and/or externally? Why?

Yes, naturally people come and also leave again.

Some people come just for a little taste of love and silence. Others deeply commit to the transformation process of the heart. Our path requires endurance.

And the transformation process itself occurs mostly in a hidden way. Only after this process, the pathless path is really understood. I am talking about our traditional training. The most important thing is that a student fully opens to the Self, the Presence from moment to moment. There are not many who fully dedicate themselves to this. I personally have never distanced myself from a spiritual friend. If someone wants to go, this is good. If someone wants to stay, this is good. Whatever helps people to awaken is good. There is no separation.

24. How much time should a student spend in observation of themselves before they commit to a teacher, and vice versa?

I observed Mrs. Tweedie for three years. This also had to do with the fact that I was engaging in a Tibetan Buddhist form of practice - however, without having found a teacher who matched my inner understanding. Karmapa would have, but he had just passed away back then.

Thus, I traveled to Mrs. Tweedie in London as often as I could. I was deeply touched by the intense silence and radiant love. And so I asked her if I could be her student.

Today I tend to speak of spiritual guidance. I prefer this description. The teacher-student relationship is subject to so many projections – positive and negative. I hold a holarchical understanding.

From a biological perspective, we are all humans – in that, we are all the same. Simultaneously, in terms of our talents, development or depth of consciousness, we are not the same. One human life may be dedicated to the arts. In that, we are not equal – I can learn from them.

Consciousness development as a way of life – this is a field in which this person, Annette, has certain competencies. What I am talking about here is our natural authority. Important in this is that we do not make value judgments.

In my understanding, the teacher-student relationship is not about attachment. If anything, it is about connection. But even that is not fully accurate; teacher and student are ultimately not-two. When there is no subject nor object, but only Reality Itself, the teacher-student relationship is fully transcendent.

The levels that we are touching on and talking about here are purely patterns of vibration in certain frequencies. Ultimately, everything is inseparably One, and within this, all these patterns of frequency dance.

25. Who assesses the teacher?

Presence is a mirror. Forms that arise in it are part of the causal level, the becoming. They are images that are reflected in the mirror. Both are not-two, yet also not the same. And so teacher is a mirror – pure Consciousness – and a reflection of that which forms, moves and changes.

It is a dance between Being und Becoming.

The more a teacher is rooted in the mirror-level, the more transparent all forms of manifestation are. They will notice all movement in conscious Being, and simultaneously transcend them.

But the teacher is also a human being – that is, imperfect. If he was perfect, Bhai Sahib, teacher of Mrs. Tweedie, said he would instantly drop dead.

The incompleteness creates friction that can evoke sudden internal or external reactions.

A wise teacher is open for all truthful reflections.

Fundamentally, life itself is the greatest guru, Mrs. Tweedie said to us.

Assessment thus continuously takes place through wakeful Being-Presence in the here and now. Even a cat, or a flower, aside from other humans, can be helpful in the process of self-reflection. Sometimes a teacher also consciously steps into contact with other teachers in order to continue learning. It requires humility and beginner's mind – throughout one's entire life, I believe.

What do you think about self-declared teachers?

You ask challenging questions! This is not easy to answer.

Ramana Maharshi, for example, had no teacher who taught him. He had a near-death experience at the age of 16 while being fully conscious. This radically changed his life.

He is and was a great teacher, unquestionably.

Eckhart Tolle and Byron Katie bring a particular force into the world, and thus, the question of whether they are self-declared is not raised.

Thus, perhaps the question should rather be: With whom does this question come up?

I believe that this is always the case when there is any lack of clarity in a teacher's way of life or the way in which they teach. A central question here is always whether they want to be a teacher, that is, whether a part is fed out of that "I", that wants to be something special. A true teacher has neither name nor face. I stand firmly in that. The most important question, however, is whether a teacher has experienced and integrated the absolute negation as well as the absolute affirmation within themselves, which is expressed in their way of life.

Mrs. Tweedie once said to us that the teacher only needs to be one step ahead. That means that every person can be a teacher.
And not only that – Mother Earth, for example, is a wonderful teacher! This makes all of us students and teachers at the same time – that is beginner's mind.

26. In a teacher-student relationship, a lot is projected onto the teacher: The mother, the friend, the partner, the therapist, etc. How does a teacher remain free of this within themselves?

Yes, a lot is projected onto a teacher. The projection can be positive or negative. Projection occurs when somebody sees an inner, not conscious, image or aspect of his own inner alchemy in another person, which pushes itself into consciousness but is not yet recognized for what it is. Through this, the person hands that part of themselves over to the other person in the form of energy. That projection can be taken back very easily, by becoming conscious of this projected part, and giving it back to oneself.
Projections that fall onto me have a subtle, energetic effect on a particular level. I sense it very well when it happens.
The taste of a positive projection is different to that of a negative one.
Yet ultimately, both are simply projections.
One projection can also change into the opposite projection, as projections are based on duality – they are mutually dependent. A

teacher is free and insusceptible to influence when no one is there. When there is no "I" and "mine", a received projection may be noticed, but it does not stick – it simply passes through me. In Being, Here and Now, there is I – transparently. There is nothing that can "get caught" in transparency. Like mist that is falling through a star.

27. Do you believe that the traditional teacher-student relationship will continue to exist in the future?

In the near future – yes and no. From a global perspective, this will depend on the culture and level of consciousness. In our cultural circle, the teacher-student relationship has already changed significantly within the last twenty years. As I already mentioned, today I speak of spiritual guidance.

Eckart Tolle once joked that the "profession" of a spiritual teacher does not have a future. At least that is what he hopes for. One should find a different profession, so he says.

There is wisdom in that. Presence is ultimately the most "natural" thing there is. Everything is Consciousness, independent of what arises or does not arise. Once we recognize this, spiritual teachers in the traditional sense are not required anymore.

28. Under which circumstances would you advise a person not to pursue a spiritual path?

This requires thorough exploration. There are very few situations in which I would advise against pursuing a spiritual path. An example would be in the case of severe psychological illness. However, it is also vital to thoroughly examine such a case, as a so called psychological illness may turn out to be a spiritual crisis at its core.

Fundamentally, it is impossible not to be spiritual.

A spiritual path opens up a deeper dimension of consciousness for a person. From an evolutionary perspective, the developing change of consciousness is inevitable. It calls a human being into deeply transformative processes, both internally and externally. As such, a spiritual path, or a pathless spiritual journey is recommendable to anyone.

It is important to understand that this is not about a path that needs to be walked but about consciousness – Presence, which always is, was and will be. It is about recognizing this within its evolutionary dynamic – however this may occur.

29. Does it make sense to you to seek a teacher from within one's own cultural circle?

This again needs to be considered on an individual basis. For some it is easier to be in contact with a teacher who is from the same cultural circle. For others it may be helpful to have a teacher from, for example, India. Ultimately, whatever supports a person to experience contact with their own inner teacher makes sense.

30. How does a teacher-student relationship begin and when does it end?

Traditionally, a teacher-student relationship begins when the student asks the teacher for spiritual guidance and the teacher accepts. A teacher-student relationship ends when Is what Is. In the nondual perspective, teacher and student are one. Yet the teacher also always has a special place in the student's heart.
This, at least, is how I feel. Mrs. Tweedie was my teacher. I feel deepest gratitude and respect for her.

31. What does a student mean to the teacher?

Everything – and nothing. The teacher only holds one interest – for the student to awaken. In this sense, they mean everything to him. And as nobody is going anywhere, they simultaneously mean nothing. There should not be any adhesion, no attachment. The entire process is about liberation. In Reality Itself there is no relationship. The existence of a relationship requires a subject and an object. In Reality Itself there is only that endless, consciousness-radiating love that is always inclusive, everybody all at once now.

32. How is knowledge imparted?

At first, knowledge is eradicated. Because true knowledge is rooted in not-knowing. In Being-Presence, true knowledge reveals itself intuitively, or through self-inquiry from out of itself. The presence of a teacher is helpful in this. Of course words and concepts are also used as a sort of finger pointing to the moon – to that which cannot be named. But there is much more. That which exists between words – Silence – is that which creates. Traditionally we say that "knowledge" is transmitted in presence with the teacher. It simply radiates.

Additionally, Mrs. Tweedie once said that the actual training occurs at night. This is related to the specific path of the Sufi. Ultimately, every person carries all knowledge within themselves. In Awareness, the access to this is free. Sometimes this knowledge is called wisdom.

33. Is it only the student who learns from the teacher – or is the student also a mirror for the teacher?

On the level of becoming we are always learning. In Becoming, evolutionary development that is rooted in Being expresses itself. Evolution has a direction – it is not arbitrary. The forms that arise as modifications of the One, inseparable Reality, are more complex and deeper in consciousness. Human beings are an expression of this. Our world has tremendously increased in complexity and richness in the last decade, and is continuing to do so. On this level, there is always something to learn, to integrate, and to adapt in terms of a global/local way of life, which is inseparably One with the acausal Reality, with Being.

This learning expresses itself on all levels: No matter if student, environment, gardens, households, family, world affairs, etc. As such, the student also serves as a reflection for the teacher, while being able to clearly differentiate between what is mirror and what is mirror-reflection, despite them being inseparably One.

Are there still students that pose a real challenge to you?

In our tradition, the student is given as much freedom as possible. The amount of contact is largely determined by the one who has asked for spiritual guidance. I ask to see people twice a year; that is the minimum for me. The challenging people are those who are lukewarm. That is, those who never fully embark on the process of heart-transformation. That complicates the inner, alchemic process. My deepest heart-wish is that these people may fully enter the fire of love. But this cannot be forced, as the person needs to be respected for who they are, without any judgment.

34. What do you advise your students in spiritual crises?

I cannot generalize that. Every person is unique. A spiritual crisis can have many different causes. There are mild spiritual crises, where a deep conversation and close companionship suffice. There can also be deep spiritual crises. However, I have never experienced this in my immediate environment. Rather, once in a while people who I have never seen before come to me during such times of spiritual crisis. Often, I then work together with other people, for example, doctors and psychiatrists, who are part of the spiritual network that was founded by Stan Grof. All levels of the human being need to be carefully examined: body, psyche, dimensions of the soul, Kundalini-energy, etc.

Do you still experience spiritual crises yourself – if so, how do you respond?

Inner growth occurs in cycles. That means that we will always encounter certain layers that need to be overcome. In my experience, however, these are not as prominent anymore as those that occur in the dark night of the soul. And yet one finds oneself in a state of feeling totally alone.
Only in hindsight I know with certainty that a "step" was right. In the moment itself it is a step into emptiness, into the unknown.

I believe however – and can feel it to some extent, that there is a collective dark night of the soul. When the heart and consciousness are open and there is a clear commitment to stand for the whole of humanity, another deep spiritual crisis may occur.

In such times of transition, which may be a better way of putting it, I remain mainly silent.

I also pray for guidance, as pale lights are mistaken all too easily for the One Light.

So I am wide awake and pay attention to the synchronicity of coherence. I do not want anything but to follow the Light of all lights.

35. To what extent is a spiritual teacher also contact person for a student's personal topics, like problems in relationship, job, family, etc.? What should they absolutely not be contacted about?

Mrs. Tweedie was simply there for people. And so am I. It may be that at a certain point in the course of a person's development, a conversation about relationship, job or family becomes important. Later, this will not be necessary anymore, as the inner alchemy is much better understood, the person is at peace with themselves, has cleaned up, forgiven – themselves and others, and is rooted more in Being.

Essentially, the spiritual path is a path for adults.

As I already mentioned, everyone is given the greatest possible freedom, so that one's self-responsibility can grow until one reaches that place where light dances in light.

For me there is nothing that cannot be talked about.

May a student criticize a teacher?

I am open for respectful constructive criticism. I am a learner.

36. Does a spiritual teacher also take time off?

On a certain level, there is no time off, as time does not exist and everything and all is simultaneously. Every person is multi-dimensional: There is a body, a psyche, the soul, the mind, the family, the job, the spiritual dimension, the world, the existence as a world-citizen, the Light of lights…

For me, all human-beings and other sentient beings are in the Heart, and on this level, there is no time off. It is as if one eye is always awake.

On the level on which time and space exist, I do take time off.

Generally that means that I retreat for about two months at the beginning of the year. I do this in order to assess myself, to listen to the silence… In Being and Becoming, which is not-two, there is no separation.

Everything is THAT, and so nobody goes anywhere. There is neither time off, nor no time off. IT IS.

On the human level I make sure that my life is as balanced as possible, so that all aspects of Being and Becoming are in harmony.

37. How were you as a student towards your teacher as a young woman?

I deeply respected Mrs. Tweedie.

In our tradition, a teacher is not worshiped. We do not put pictures up or anything like that. The teacher has no face and no name. There was simply a very natural and deep respect.

The relationship towards the teacher is, in itself, a highly complex matter.

There was something in me that was always present in respect, wide awake and very attentive. I deeply absorbed every gesture, every word into my heart. I wrote Mrs. Tweedie about everything, really everything that moved me inside.

Sometimes she answered, sometimes she didn't – it did not matter. I only wanted one thing: To go home – that is what I called it back then.

Soon I learnt that this attention, this wakeful Being-Presence is inherent to every human being. In each person I saw two beings – in essence, Mrs. Tweedie.

38. How are teacher-student relationships today, compared to the time when you were Mrs. Tweedie's student?

The teacher-student relationship has changed tremendously. Mrs. Tweedie was not allowed to speak the name of her teacher out loud. We, on the other hand, were allowed to call Mrs. Tweedie, Mrs. Tweedie. I am addressed as Annette. Even though this is an external matter, it reflects a distinctive change: Today, teachers and students are approaching each other, meaning that the consciousness-level of the whole of humanity has increased. The mystic dimension of the Unio Mystica is taking place from moment to moment, now. This is a r(evolution) in the spiritual sense, which is exceptional in the history of humanity.

That means that in a deep sense, we do not require any spiritual paths. Instead, this moment reveals itself as a gateway into conscious Being, in which all Becoming occurs. That is a quantum leap!

Will the "spiritual Great Self" be our teacher in the future?

Traditionally we say that the external teacher should always point to the inner teacher. Every person has an inner entity that knows, beyond that which we normally understand as knowledge. We have always been what we believe to find: That. I would not call it "spiritual Great Self". It is Reality Itself.

39. Can you say something about your relationship with Mrs. Tweedie, and how it changed over the course of time?

Mrs. Tweedie is and was my teacher. I owe everything to her – she was my gateway into Being-Presence. Through her, the love that simply Is was awakened. It means being in love without knowing with what or whom. And of course it is not the person herself who evokes this, but the Silence and Presence.

We do not worship the teacher. We simply respect and hold deep gratitude in our heart that is always present. Mrs. Tweedie let us partake in her life. She was not complete, and transparently so, so that we as students were able to mature. We could see a hint of shadow, did not need to close our eyes to it, and saw her greatness, her guiding role. She truly surrendered. Her Presence and wisdom radiated in silence. She had an understanding for every human concern. Everything was welcomed.

Mrs. Tweedie showed us the gateway through the YOU. The truth – THAT – was the inner beloved. The longing in our hearts led us into the Unio Mystica, which is everything and nothing at once. In my further development I focused on the gate of the "I am", of which Ramana Maharshi and Nisargadatta Maharaj were such clear living examples. My earlier connections to the Indian roots taught me to worship the Earth, the perfection of manifestation. Life circumstances forced me to go even deeper, which illuminated the inner experience of the All-Nothing in a way that transcended and simultaneously included the Sufi Tradition. I found myself in the next holon, where all spiritual traditions unite in THAT. And the learning continues.

Today I understand that the spiritual dimension of human existence is something totally natural. There will come a time in which it will inherently shape our human life. This is an evolutionary perspective, as Theilhard de Chardin, Jean Gebser and especially Sri Aurobindo, and the Mother have conveyed.

The Becoming in Being will increase in meaning. It is about the foundation of a new civilization of all of humanity. At the moment I receive important inspiration from Adi Da – which needs to be treated differentially though. Ken Wilber has also conveyed essential insights regarding an integral perspective. I take the liberty of bringing the best of all wisdom together, in order for us humans to be able to take the next step in consciousness. Thus, a lot has changed and simultaneously also nothing has, as the first step remains to be the transcendence of ego, which happens now, from moment to moment.

I was gifted the inner certainty that all of this is also supported by Mrs.Tweedie and Bhai Sahib, and with them, by the entire Sufi lineage. That is an inexpressible gift for me.

My purpose is being a carrier of light. Every person has not only a worldly, but also a spiritual purpose. What this is also depends on the culture and time frame in which a person lives, because it is in line with the need of the evolutionary development of the world.

Esoteric work that occurs in more hidden ways also contributes. We know, for example, of people who meditate in the Himalayas. We do not know who they are – and yet their way of being in this life contributes to holding the world together.

In this way, the task of a light carrier is also not necessarily obvious. It is very subtle, and yet I know that in this lies my contribution to the whole. Mrs. Tweedie was the "bell ringer". She reminded us to recognize what we truly are – Consciousness – whatever may arise or not. There is only THAT, the One Reality, self-radiant, self-revealing, self-correcting, and arising in it modifications of that One Reality, which come and go – inseparably One.

Questions about
the World

40. In the light of the present state of the world, what is the most urgent thing that we should address?

To love. To love without limitations – unconditionally – as an awakened being, Here and Now, where Being and Becoming are known as inseparable Unity. This is a way of living that contributes to the total harmony of the Kosmos, to the well-being of everybody all at once, and thereby lays the foundation for a new civilization.

What does the world mean to you?

The world in Presence, which is where I am right now, is pure wonder. The wind is singing, the blades of grass are dancing in it, the bees are humming; there is a radiance in everything, which is simultaneously transparent. In One All-Being the world is what it is: Reflections in consciousness, full of colors, flavors and forms, which come and go. At the same time I am fully aware with compassion of the actual state of our World.

Of course, when I focus on the world in its present, external state, it is at the edge of destruction.

It is not planet Earth that is destroying itself. It is us human beings who are destroying the natural, cosmic-systemic balance on Earth. And that is a real threat today. What is required is a change of consciousness, out of which a way of life can emerge for every human-being that is rooted in the WE, in cooperation and tolerance, for the well-being of all life.

The world is very precious to me. In view of the entire universe, however, it is nothing. That is the paradox. But this allows me to actively take a stand for this world, unintentionally/intentionally, in joy and serenity.

41. How has your view on the world changed in the course of your life?

Yes, my view on the world has changed.

On the one hand, the spiritual training has given me access to really seeing what IS.

Only through present-moment awareness, the beauty that the Earth reflects is fully revealed to us human beings. She is unique.

Also, my horizon is continuously expanding. The entire world, that is, everything and all at once, is contained in wakeful Being-Presence – indeed, is part of the true Reality. This is means to hold a cosmo-centric world perspective.

42. Which role does humanity play in the world today, and what is your perception of its purpose?

The human race is the crucial point in today's world process.

It is in human consciousness that evolution occurs today. If we get stuck in the identification of "I" and "mine", a separating perspective, we will succumb to the fight for resources, energies, etc. That is not intelligent.

We can only meet the challenges of today constructively, if we understand that we are one species – humanity itself, inseparably One. On a consciousness-level, this means a quantum leap.

On a practical level, this means that we approach problems from the zero-point, and represent humanity as a whole. A zero-vantage point means that we are rooted in conscious Being, in Prior Unity. We meet each other from human to human without carrying flags, like I am green or red or Catholic or Muslim, rich or poor – respecting the uniqueness of each and all. We advocate the inseparable Unity of all that is. We see the whole, not the "I" or the "mine" or an ethnocentric perspective. The inseparable One has an intrinsic desire for cooperation, and is tolerant and respectful towards all differences. In this way it becomes possible for humanity to re-experience harmony with the whole, a higher cosmic order.

43. Which purpose does spirituality serve today?

Spirituality is very essential. As Sartre already expressed: That, which says "I am", is not the same consciousness that thinks. Spirituality opens the door to the One Reality, which can, among other ways, be described as "I am". That is a crucial difference; from "I am Karl" to "I am – conscious Being everybody all at once, and nothing at all at the same time".

As already described, consciousness itself has not yet been extensively investigated. In consciousness lie "qualities" for which we are only now discovering an adequate language. The gifts of thinking, feeling etc. are not meant to be eradicated through this – instead, they finally receive their true place.

Human beings do not only inherently carry the gift of self-reflection – they are in essence pure Consciousness. This is a completely new dimension, which may literally turn the world upside down. Today, humanity lives a life that is mostly governed by the idea of separation. And that produces fear. It is fear of the others, the unknown, of change, etc. Spirituality can reveal a deeper dimension of existence to humanity, in so far as we recognize the inseparable existence of all Being. The foundation for this development is love. Love is inherent in Presence and can become the foundation for co-existence and the well-being of all.

44. What responsibilities does a spiritual teacher/ student have today with regards to the world?

A spiritual teacher should lead the way. That means that they live what they speak.

In this day and age this requires development on the horizontal as well as the vertical lines of consciousness. On the one hand it is about holding a nondual perspective in present, wakeful Beingness, on the other hand it is about adapting a cosmocentric way of life. Therefore, I am active in many different areas. For example, the organization "Open Hands" that I am involved in has been supporting projects in the Third World for more than 25 years now.

My commitment begins within the close circle of family and partnership, grows into the field of the two spiritual centers that I am leading spiritually, into cooperation with, for example, the Integral Movement and the magazine Evolve, and flows into the heart-matter on a global level, where it is about the birthing of the Forum for Universal Cooperation.

The commitment is rooted in a doing in not-doing. Despite being deeply involved, I want nothing. It is intentional/unintentional. In that there is no should and no must. The impulses arise from the love of the heart – just like that.

It is about a freely chosen responsibility that creates Becoming for the well-being of all, and which is in harmony with life.

Students, too, will develop this lived spirituality from within themselves.

It is an evolutionary necessity, so to speak.

45. Does life-long inner work even make sense anymore when considering the state of our external world?

The outer state of the world is a reflection of the inner state of the human beings. Everything is connected to everything. This is not a utopia. The world that is causally determined follows certain universal laws: plants, animals, human beings die, for example – that means their bodies come and go. That is likely going to stay this way for the time being. We can see a principal of sacrifice in this; plants serve the animals, bacteria serve the human body, etc. The "sacrifice" that is required from us human beings is to let go of the I-identification, that means, undoing the knots of self-contraction. When enough people understand and experience this, and are able to root it "sustainably" in conscious Being from moment to moment, we will see it reflected in the outer world.

I was pleasantly surprised to read in the German newspaper "Süddeutsche Zeitung" that it is indeed possible to produce renewable energies for all of Europe. Presently, it is not the lack of know-how, but the egocentrism of single nations, which inhibits cooperation. Recognizing the true problem marks the beginning of change.

46. How, in your opinion, can one make spiritual thinking and acting accessible to young people?

Young people are of particular importance to me. Very often, young people have a feeling-sense that is in harmony with the whole. One can meet the youth where they stand. Our language has to be adapted, without losing its essence.

Being a role model to the youth is important, I believe. They often have a clear sense of what is truthful and what is not. And ultimately, it is loving them, unconditionally, that touches their heart. In this, a sharing and recognizing of the deepest purpose of being human begins.

In former times, the youth mostly learnt from the elders. I have a sense that we may have entered a different era for the first time. On the level of consciousness, the elders can learn incredibly much from the younger people. They seem to be equipped with a very uncontracted and deeply holistic consciousness. What do you think?

Yes, there are more and more young people who carry a deep knowledge within themselves.
That is wonderful. I am simultaneously noticing that older people are respected for their life-experience, their path, their life-wisdom. A new cooperation emerges.

47. Spirituality is often still lived in silence and in secrecy. Do you consider this to be in keeping with the current times?

There can be a phase in the spiritual process in which retreating into a more silent space is appropriate, so that a newly birthed plant has the chance to grow strong roots. When this has taken place, however, I believe that the time has come to speak in public about this dimension, this Reality. I often encounter people who are deeply spiritual in their private lives, but who hardly dare to express this in, for example, their professional environment. The time has come to speak freely and openly about love and wisdom – of a love that is all-inclusive, and a wisdom, which, as an inner knowledge, is inherent in every human being. What I am talking about is almost a form of spiritual "outing". It means also openly standing for One World.

48. Cooperation and the new, inner understanding of a world citizenship is one of the topics of our time and in a way, most spiritual teachers' central statement. How can I understand the way in which spiritual teachers engage with one another? We are talking here about people with hopefully mostly ego-freed personalities. What is the lived reality with regards to cooperation?

Cooperation and tolerance are central in today's world, globally on all levels. The spiritual teachers have not practiced this much up until now. It is a new field. And of course I am of the opinion that spiritual teachers should lead the way here. Thus far, there have been many trans-confessional dialogues. But cooperation means much more to me. It is a finding each other in the next higher holon, in a sort of meta-sangha, in a conscious WE.

There is, for example, the Global Oneness Day and the Planetary Birthday. Another emergence is Global Spirituality, in which a joint language was developed out of seven different religious traditions – a language that could serve as a foundation for a religion, which carries the essence of all religions, so to speak. Amma was the first to call this a religion of love.

Spiritual teachers also need to learn real cooperation, in which their own school is included and transcended. With the interdisciplinary program Menschen in Spirit, which was initiated in 2013 at Villa Unspunnen, we developed a project that both facilitates the meta-sangha of teachers, and aspires to true cooperation on the content-level. It is not about certain people or specific organizations anymore, but about collaboration within the next holon.

49. If you could immediately change something in the world, what would it be?

Firstly, it is important to understand what the world is and what the occurring orders are on the different levels of existence. It is not about a utopia. The world of forms comes and goes. They are light-reflections on the mirror. The most important thing for us human beings is Reality Itself, which inherently radiates in love. That is the most important thing today.

Please, three things!

Deepest peace
Unity
All-love

Personal Questions

50. **You are not just a spiritual teacher – you are also mother of two children, entrepreneur (you lead two big seminar houses) and many people work with and for you, you are in a relationship, travel a lot and give presentations, hold retreats and seminars, write books, give Tai-Chi training and various other trainings, are interested in new developments in the fields of physics, neuroscience, politics, history, technology,...and much more.**

How do you manage to do all this?

By living every moment in Presence. I let my heart guide the way, do not want anything personally, simply go with the flow of life, awake, present, loving. I read the signs of life and learn. I am rooted in beginner's mind and take time to retreat every year, in order to fundamentally assess and deeply listen to what IT wants. My life-energy is largely free and can therefore flow into that which is right now. I go with that which gives joy to my innermost being. I am enthusiastic about what I do, and that lights the spark in others. I hardly require any energy anymore around the Me and I. That leaves a lot of energy for the whole. I take good care of myself, physically, psychologically, on all levels. I am a friend to myself and through that, to all human beings on a deep level. A lot becomes possible through this way of being.

Are you ambitious?

Mrs. Tweedie said to me one day: "We are successful". That made me listen up, as I had understood success mainly in the societal context. That was a learning opportunity for me. Success in the worldly sense I do not strive for. When I deeply reflect on your question, I sense a certain mixed field. There can also be spiritual ambition in the subtle and causal spheres of existence. You know, holding an evolutionary tension on a particular level of consciousness may be what this is about for me. Wanting nothing, absolutely nothing, while simultaneously being totally receptive and going with the emerging flow of evolution. Having a clear direction is not necessarily linked to ambition. And it is a good question for self-inquiry.

51.   What makes you happy?

Happiness that is inherent in Being – in the moment – is happiness for me.

External happiness that is based on contingencies comes and goes. I just enjoy it when something comes to me, which fills me with joy, for example a flower bouquet, a special dream, etc. But I also know that the flowers will wilt, and that the dream itself fades away. I am happy when my children are happy and I am happy when George and I look each other in the eyes. All these are gifts of life for me. What makes me most happy is when people awaken. That is my greatest joy in this world. And sometimes I can clearly see that a single step someone is making is one that will fundamentally change their life. Then I experience deep joy for this person.

52.   Here's a question raised by Max Frisch: Have you already managed to get to know your children, that is, not to see them as son and daughter?

Yes, there are moments in which I do manage this. But then there are times where I am fully mom, until I remember the vastness of the sky. Then our conversations become freer, in deep love – they shine.

53.   What have you learnt from your children?

Especially during delivery and their infant years, my children were my greatest teachers. They taught me to be there for them. I am not a mother type, and so this was a great challenge for me. Through this, they taught me to direct my attention towards something different, something greater than me. They taught me to discover the world anew.

They challenged a lot of my conceptions about how girls and boys in a civilized environment are supposed to be. They taught me to love unconditionally and to feel the fragility of being human. They taught me a new togetherness, in which everyone has their place. They taught me to grieve when my marriage ended. They taught me to be truthful, as they saw through all the adult playacting. And finally, they taught me to let them go. That means to love in such a way that the love leaves the attachment behind. I could go on and on. They were and are my greatest teachers in this life. I thank you so much for your existence.

54. What was the most important step of your life?

I believe that the most important step in my life was to give myself fully to the spiritual path, to the One Reality.

Here is a very personal question in relation to this: In nearly every profession that I know, one has the possibility to develop oneself in the course of one's life, to change something, to quit. One always stays a spiritual teacher, though. How do you deal with this great vocation, which is simultaneously a commitment?

By not thinking but being – and if anything, thinking from this state of Being. Now – just like that.
In the Here and Now, all of this does not exist. Every moment is new – there is no time in that. Where there is no time, there are also no longstanding commitments. In this way, space to breathe, space for the soul, and freedom can emerge.

55. Which roles do friendships play in your life?

I assume that you mean friendship itself, and not the term "being among friends" as sanghas and spiritual communities are called in the Sufi tradition. My greatest friend is my husband. I can share, exchange and explore a lot with him. My now adult children are also friends to me, although naturally in a different way, due to our systemic constellation.

And then there is a wider circle of people, with whom I share the essentials in life, who work, live and act with me. But in the depth of my heart, every person is ultimately a friend, also all animals and plants, Mother Earth, the stars, the sky, infinity.

56.   Who would you rather not have met?

There is no one who I would have rather not met. As from all encounters, the so called positive or negative ones, I was able to learn a lot. In hindsight I can only feel gratitude. They have all contributed to me being who I am today.
Are there any people you feel the world would have been better off without? For example for causing great suffering and misery?

This question cannot be answered as such. Of course, from a common sense point of view, how can the actions of Adolf Hitler, Pol Pot, Saddam Hussein etc. be justified in any way?
These men have caused so much suffering with the support of many others.
I wish that humanity had been spared this. But we need to inquire deeper; how can it happen that an intelligent nation such as Germany handed the power over to Adolf Hitler? Which collective and individual patterns play a role here? And what is the true cause of suffering? It is really the ignorance of human-beings.
That is why the shift in consciousness is such a central topic.

57.   What do you still want to learn – and what not?

One part of me is curious like a child. I am open and happy to learn and discover new things.
Thus, I am interested to go even deeper into the field of consciousness, to explore the cosmocentric perspective as a way of life, as well as our possibilities as co-creators. Likewise, I am interested in scientific insights and new technologies.

Apart from that, I do not ask myself this question. If there is something to learn, there is something to learn. If not, not. The Presence is intelligent enough to know, where the path leads. I am particularly interested in accessing knowledge that exists without needing to be learned – and simultaneously living on this Earth with good common sense and learning what is there to be learned.

58. What is your greatest wish?

That humanity awakens.

You've got one more…

That humanity awakens!

59. Why is it such a challenge for us to love in relationships?

Love in Being-Presence is unconditional by nature.
That means it loves fundamentally, without limitations. When we talk about love, we say for example: "I really love vegetables", or "I love my cat, I love my children, my home, my dog, my village community, Africa, the world." We can see that the field of love is continuously expanding.
It expands from the I, the we, into the ethnocentric, the worldcentric, all the way into a cosmocentric consciousness.
The wider and more encompassing love is, the more transparent the "I" and the "Mine" become in it. In Being-Presence there is only I-strength, but no identified I anymore: IT loves from out of itself everything and all at once in Consciousness, which is simultaneously empty.
Romantic relationships are often a great challenge for us people in the Western world. We project the so called love onto the partner. With this go expectations, hopes, attachments etc. It is unbelievable how many things a partner is supposed to be for us: lover, father

or mother, interesting, intelligent, athletic, successful, sophisticated, and at the same time good in household matters, etc.

Nobody can fulfill all these expectations. Relationships are a field of great projections. C. G. Jung described four steps of love: 1. being in love, the archaic stage; 2. the stage in which we become aware about the extent to which we have projected onto our partner, and take this back; 3. the stage in which we work out closeness and distance, so that both people can develop themselves according to their nature; and 4.unconditional love.

So it takes a maturation process of the love in the relationship with your partner. Those who love unconditionally know that they themselves are the love that they used to wish to receive from their partner. That radically changes the partnership: It is no longer based on the principal of lack, but that of wholeness. The word relationship receives a different meaning and becomes lighter and transparent.

Ultimately, the word relationship falls away. Only when something is separated there can be relationship – it takes two who relate to each other. In the fourth step of love C. G. Jung speaks about the unconditional love. What is meant by that? In Becoming, the relative level, there is an intense expression of love – something that we do not share with just anyone. But the Being-love is there for everything and all at once. In this we encounter another paradox.

I can best explain this with the example of my own children. The All-Love loves every child on Earth. And so my heart is touched by every child that is hungry, sick, or suffering hardship, and delighted by every laughing child on Earth. And I do what needs to be done in order to reduce the hunger, hardship and sickness of all children. When my child is sick there is an added dimension: I make tea, take the temperature, sit at the side of the bed, etc. Both aspects exist.

60. Which character traits do you value most in other people – which ones the least? Which character traits do you value most about yourself – which ones the least?

Truthfulness, humor, authentic being and all-encompassing love. These characteristics are a gift to humanity. So-called bad characteristics are rooted in ignorance.
What do I value about myself? The love that IS, the wisdom that resonates in it, radiant Consciousness. But those are not personal traits, but transpersonal in the sense that they are inherent to all human beings in wakeful Being. I am also not perfect. I am not yet free of certain habits and still discover shadow aspects within myself. And that doesn't matter. Beginners mind!

61. Do you like being a woman? And what does it mean for you to be a woman?

I very much like being a woman. As a woman I enter life with a certain tone, a certain dress, which is complementary to the male dress and tone.
I love the tone that sounds in this dress: That can be mother, lover, that which carries the wildness of the yogini within itself, that which can embody heaven and Earth.
I wear this dress with respect and deep love for that, which is: A divine expression of the One.

62. Do you think that as a woman you can understand men?

Nowadays, scientific findings show that we – no matter if man or woman –are always a certain mix of both sexes, sometimes more, sometimes less. Mrs. Tweedie once told us that it is almost impossible to understand the other sex in all its depth. I cannot conclusively answer this question. To me, every human-being is unique and simultaneously carries a secret within themselves. It is important to respect this secret in the other person.

That means that the man himself does occasionally remain a secret to you?

Yes. And in that lies beauty.

63. What does it mean for a child to have a spiritual teacher as a mother? And what, do you think, does it mean for a partner?

This question should really be answered by my son and my daughter. From my perspective, it was good for all of us. As when the love in the heart expands, it leaves more room for the development of every unique being, especially also within the family. Looking at our partnership as a whole, it is a blessing for us.

Love is capable of everything when it can give itself freely.

64. Which type of person would you like to get to know? Why?

I would like to get to know all people that think and act cosmo-centrically, as well as all creative and scientific minds who contribute specifically and substantially to the realization of the One World – on the foundation of Prior Unity.

65. Are you a good friend to yourself? And if so, when did this begin?

Yes, today I am a good friend to myself. It took some time until I had integrated all aspects of human existence to a great extent, and learnt to appreciate them. That is part of awakening: Being a friend to yourself. Through that all other people become friends in essence.

66. What is the most important book for you and why?

The most important book for me is the book with completely empty pages. An empty book contains all possibilities.

67. What is beauty for you? And what does it mean to you?

Beauty is a fundamental attribute of our universe. For me, the starlit sky is beautiful, a blade of grass in the wind, the entire Earth is beautiful, every pair of eyes, the babbling of a mountain brook... Beauty is above, below, left and right, inside and out – it is everywhere.
And of course it is our duty to see this beauty, to cultivate it, indeed, to contribute to it.
Beauty helps me. It reminds me of the inherently exiting beauty, of the preciousness of every moment.

68. What can you only bear with a sense of humor?

Everything and nothing.

Vision

69. What is your vision for the way in which human beings will live together in the future?

Sri Aurobindo was a source of deep inspiration for me regarding this. I can see the evolutionary development of humanity in front of my inner eye, and I recognize a development of consciousness in that.

This development is twofold; on the one hand, more and more people recognize the Unio Mystica in Presence, which results in a nondual understanding. On the other hand, consciousness develops from an archaic to a mythic to a rational to an integral level. Ken Wilber has contributed substantially to this understanding. Deep enlightenment today can be understood as nondual, cosmocentric consciousness that expresses itself as a way of life. It is an evolutionary perspective based on a holistic worldview. At the beginning of the 20th Century, Sri Aurobindo already spoke about the further evolutionary consciousness development of humanity. His words give a taste of this. He writes in "The Divine Life":

"The gnostic individual would be in the world and of the world, but would also exceed it in his consciousness and live in his self of transcendence above it; he would be universal but free in the universe, individual but not limited by a separative individuality. The True Person is not an isolated entity, his individuality is universal; for he individualizes the universe."

"Into all his acts the inner oneness, the inner communion will attend him and enter into his relations with others, who will not be to him others but selves of himself in the one existence, his own universal existence."

"For the complete individual is the cosmic individual, since only when we have taken the universe into ourselves - and transcended it - can our individuality be complete."

"His feeling of universality, his action of universality will be always a spontaneous state and natural movement, an automatic expression of the Truth, an act of the joy of the spirit's self-existence."

In other words, it is about recognizing ourselves as an inseparable Unity, which is, was and will be above all differences. This will enable us to experience ourselves as one humanity on the consciousness-level. As an individual, we begin to feel, think, speak and act for the entirety of humanity. The precondition for this is a zero-point understanding in the sense that the identified I is transparent. We are Consciousness, in which everything and all arises simultaneously. When we recognize this, we cannot exploit each other anymore, cause each other harm, leave parts of our population to starve etc. The animals are also our brothers and sisters, just as the plant kingdom is part of the whole. We can meet in wisdom and love, as Self in Self, which gives first priority to the greater good. The individual integrates into the whole.

An illustration for this: An individual human being can symbolically be seen as a cell. The body cell is a Unity in itself. At the same time, it is, for example, part of a group of similarly functioning cells. There are 10,000 cells that form the sinus node of the heart. Although every cell is unique, the synchronicity of all cells together produces the electromagnetic impulse of the heart beat. Together they form a greater whole, without losing their individuality.

Similarly, the individual could integrate into the noosphere, that is, the consciousness of humanity as a whole.

70. How do you see the inner and outer development of human beings in the future?

The inner development cannot be separated from the outer development. There is only THAT. Development in human beings means to recognize consciousness as that which it IS. That is a silent (r)evolution that brings a lot with it. In this, there is recognition of that which exists eternally without change, and for the Becoming, the continuously changing that arises within it.

The ever changing coming and going evolutionary way of manifestation takes place within the unchanging One Reality. It is like the wave that is the ocean. This is how we can understand the dual basis of the true Unity. The external development of human beings, of humanity as a whole, expresses itself collectively in the area of politics, society, economics, culture, technology and science. Here it is always about progress, that is, about ensuring better chances of survival and greater well-being for human beings on Earth.

The inner development of human beings is always about transcendence, which manifests itself collectively as spirituality beyond all religions, and a philosophical and artistic culture.

The synergy of these two collective human realms is the imperative, common foundation for a truly humane, political, social and cultural life that rests upon the Prior Unity as an inseparable process.

71. What are the values of a new global consciousness, especially in ways of being with one another and in the professional context?

The new horizon is rooted in Prior Unity that includes everything and everybody at once. It is important to define specific values in relation to this. We are still at the beginning here – it is a new task for the entirety of humanity that never existed before.

We can already see first steps in the consideration of common goods: who owns the water, the natural resources, etc.? We all know that our past understanding and our largely ethnocentric behavior cannot solve the global problems for the well-being of all.

As I mentioned earlier, there are also energy concepts that could facilitate renewable energy supplies for all of Europe, if egoistic motives were not in play to prevent this from happening.

Thus, at the point in time that we are currently at, globally/locally, it is not primarily about small changes such as improvements in values at the workplace.

Of course such changes are welcome, but it is about a much more fundamental dimension:

One world or none.

So what are the specific values? Interestingly, we all know them: freedom, equality, brother and sisterhood, or love your neighbor as yourself, or the ten commandments, the ethical rules of the eightfold yoga path (for example the ahimsa principle), not to kill any living beings, right speech and behavior, etc.

So the values are familiar to us. The problem, as I see it, is that we don't live them. Why? I have given the answer to this many times. It is a matter of consciousness.

72. Can you say something about the required changes in political structures —nationally and globally, from your perspective?

Political structures are often tied to personal and political power interests, and have long ceased serving the well-being of all. Figures show that politics around the world are increasingly governed by money and power. Money is increasingly concentrating itself in the hands of a select few individuals and major corporations, thus in a sense undermining the very meaning and purpose. And this occurs even though money itself is useful, and was originally intended to contribute to the good of all.

With the introduction of interest and the handing down of money through generations, something entered our monetary system that eventually had a detrimental impact. We need wise people in politics today who cannot be bribed with power, money, sex and possessions. We need politicians who represent the whole of humanity and think and act locally/globally. We need politicians who have largely transcended their own fears, and are called from their love for the One World to accept this position. I know we are still far away from this. But I express this visionary thought very intentionally. May a first seed find its way into our hearts and unfold its affective power there, until it becomes action.

It is important for me to clarify that I am not speaking about a moral aspect that is based on shoulds or musts. It is about a conscious being human, and a freely accepted responsibility for the whole while being a part of it.

73. How can we human-beings treat our environment and nature differently?

First we should clarify our understanding of the word environment.

In German, environment means "Umwelt", which can be translated as "surrounding world". This raises a question; what do we see as the center, around which the surrounding world forms itself? In the inseparable Unity of all Being, there is no "surrounding world" – just One World – one Consciousness, and arising within it, the causally defined, manifesting world, as modifications of the One.

Love is inherent in the One Being from moment to moment. Love embraces and includes nature, and the entire Earth. It "speaks" with nature, listens to the cosmic order and opens itself more and more to a way of life locally/globally that is in harmony with the whole. I do not see a step backwards in this, but a simple way of life for the individual and the collective that creates intelligently and enables a life of dignity for everyone. We already have a lot of the right technology for this. There are so many wonderful approaches around the world. Let us come together and share the most effective knowledge and know-how at the communal table, in order to choose, from the zero-point, what best served the good of the entire humanity, regardless of who and where these ideas and developments originated from. In this way, I imagine that we can produce global solutions. The key is the consciousness of everything and all at once.

74. Our resources are becoming increasingly scarce. What are your thoughts about this?

Yes, the resources are becoming increasingly scarce. What is happening today on a global scale is that most nations try to secure as many resources as possible for their own people. But this inevitably occurs at the expense of others. Up until now, we have responded to such developments with war. That is not necessary anymore. We now have the possibility to make a different choice – to find solutions in togetherness. This requires a change in consciousness.

We already know how intricately interdependent and interconnected everything is. A financial crisis in the USA causes a financial Earthquake worldwide. Climate change does not respect national borders. These realizations can help us to become farsighted, yes, so farsighted that we can develop a global perspective.

And yet the fundamental questions remains: Who do the natural resources belong to? Could they not be a common good? And is there, from this perspective, not a way in which resources can be utilized for the good of all? These are questions that interest me.

75. Here is a question related to a totally different field: what is your perspective on the upbringing of our children, especially in public institutions, like schools and kindergartens?

The upbringing of our children is a fundamentally important topic. Looking at our educational system in Switzerland, I guess one can say that it is good in a conventional sense. But also in this regard I have fundamental questions: What are we raising our children to be? What are they supposed to learn? Is it about acquiring as much information as possible and combining it intelligently? Do we also teach them to be human, to be conscious world-citizens? Our education system primarily trains the left part of the brain – the analytic side. Holistic awareness is rarely encouraged. The result of this are one-dimensionally schooled young people.

I believe that our public education institutions should be re-structured. There are already many different approaches, which teach children in a holistic way, for example in Waldorf schools. These approaches and experiences can be drawn from. Yet in general, new values and foundations are required in the field of education. It would be an education that builds upon the inseparable Unity of all Being, which nurtures consciousness, explores and schools thinking and reason and the world of emotions, as well as supports the Unique Self of every single human being. With that I mean the authentic Self, which lives a life in integrity, in the joy of Being, and can creatively contribute to the greater good. Auroville is interesting in this regard – and not just in terms of education, but for its entire approach to life.

76. Which potential changes do you see in the working environment?

The working environment is a further field of reformation. In the Western World we have the phenomenon that those who are able to work are overloaded, while another part of the population capable of work is unemployed. And this trend will still increase. Human beings are doers by nature. We love being creative. It is inherent to us, even if we may not call this work. Expressing ourselves in our unique ways in order to contribute to the greater good is our fundamental right and simultaneously our obligation. Ideally, every human being would spend 5 hours daily contributing to the greater good, leaving the rest of the day for personal development and growth.

I know that at the moment this is far from the apparent reality. And yet, it could be a guideline. How we can implement this on a practical level, I do not know yet. What is surely required are transitions, and every step in the right direction is helpful. In today's working world, every person could benefit from relaxation and concentration training, the experience of the Power of Now, and personal shadow work. In this way, the working world can relax. But to me, this is simply a first step. Of course it is about establishing a true balance in all areas of life. Understanding this requires an inner listening. In silence an inherent ethic reveals itself that is in correspondence with the greater good.

77. And in the field of relationships and families?

Relationship and family are a further area. What we can observe is that our Western society can be characterized as hyper-individualistic. Presumably there will soon be more singles than families. Every household has a washing machine, perhaps a dishwasher, various equipment, takes up living space, etc. As an organizational principle of society, this is very wasteful. If every human being claimed this way of life, it would require multiple Earths in terms of the energy, resources, soil, etc. So I believe that there will be a trend towards mature, autonomous communities, where multiple relationships can form, which, within the consciousness of the All-One, are organized in wisdom and love. The single-existence does not correspond to our true nature. We are social beings. Deep down inside, we love being in relationship with one another. It is just that our conception of lack has led us to experience a lot of suffering in relationship, which has taught us to withdraw from one another. Moreover, it was an important step in human development for the individual to differentiate. This time is coming to an end. We are becoming more adult and mature in order to meet each other in togetherness on a new level. This will change and enrich the family and relationship structure.

78. How can we be more conscious with ourselves, with our body, our soul?

We humans are highly complex beings living a multidimensional existence. We are a body, a soul, a mind, feelings, are social beings and part of nature. Bringing all these levels of existence into harmony is the challenge that is posed in consciousness today. Respecting and cultivating the body is part of this. Keeping the body in good condition and choosing good food is essential. The food that we consume has a much greater impact than is generally known. This begins with its cultivation. Organic food should be favored, meat ideally not eaten at all, or only in moderation – also in consideration of the world food system and the animals who are living creatures. Fruits, vegetables – raw or cooked – a few nuts, etc. are good for the body. The way we cook and eat is also not trivial. Everything affects everything.

The mind should be calmed in the Now, from moment to moment. Through this it becomes peaceful and creative. It also becomes more refined, so it can intuitively open to insights. We observe our feelings.

We let them arise and ride their strength in awareness of the present moment. In this way, they do not overwhelm us anymore. They become a friend. We give our soul space, listen to what it wants. It represents the desires of our deepest being, the unique divine expression that can contribute to the greater good. In the social field, we let ourselves be guided from the heart-space, carried by the love that is everything and all at once. With nature we are connected through the One All-Being. We listen carefully to nature, walk in communion with her in Presence, from moment to moment, and enjoy the beauty and reflection of the cosmic harmony. All this is possible, Now – just like that.

Spirituality and Science

79. **Lately there has been an incredibly strong interest in spirituality from a neuroscientific perspective. There is also great interest in findings from the field of quantum physics, and literature in this field is booming. Books, presentations, and CDs are being absorbed by many people. How do you explain this great scientific interest in spirituality, and also the great demand from listeners and readers?**

Yes, in a certain way science and spirituality are approaching each other. That is excellent. There are scientists who are interested in spirituality, and of course many spiritual people are interested in the insights generated through science. Quantum physics, astronomy, and other scientific areas have, as far as I can tell, made quantum leaps in their research. Our conventional, scientific understanding has expanded tremendously as a result of that, and opens the space for deep inquiries, like, for example: What is spirit? What is consciousness? Can consciousness be localized? What, ultimately, is matter? All these questions have not been conclusively answered, just as the question of what was before the Big Bang. In our Western culture, which is still largely rooted in the rational level of consciousness and defines itself through reason and rationality, scientific insights are very helpful, especially when new insights shake the old mechanic Newtonian world view.

In their explorations of the self – the subject – the deep introspection of mystics across all traditions has lead to the identical realization – that form is emptiness and emptiness is form.

Science explores the object, for example matter, and comes to the conclusion that 99.9999% of it is empty. The work of quantum physics is of particular interest here. However, I lack grounded knowledge in this field, and thus cannot speak precisely about it.

80. **Many Buddhists place great importance on collaboration with scientists. Some make themselves available for scientific testing of certain brain regions in fMRI scanners, in order to help shed light on the secrets of inner peace, mindfulness and empathy. What is your opinion about this form of collaboration and research?**

I generally believe that all attempts that bring spirituality and science closer together are very sensible and in accordance with the zeitgeist. Again, findings within quantum physics are also a highly interesting in relation to questions about human consciousness. And if these fields can cross-fertilize each other more and more, I believe this to be very valuable.

Especially in our Western world, it seems as if everything needs to receive a scientific underpinning and proof in order for it to be approved and accepted. Don't you think that spirituality in a way supports this form of reasoning?
I believe this to be a question of conduct. When the Dalai Lama makes himself available for scientific testing, his primary intent is not to prove anything, but to open up scientific access to the spiritual dimension. When fields reach the limits of their perspectives, this can lead to dialogue, which can result in greater consciousness and understanding.

81. **Must and should a mystic path prove its deep secrets scientifically?**

A mystic who carries deep secrets would, if he was asked, make himself available to science in service of the entire evolutionary development.

82. Do you believe that God wants to be proven scientifically?

What is science? What are its recognitions based on? Fundamentally, science works with the understanding of separation between subject and object, that is, the scientist – the subject – investigates an object. That produces separation. Their findings will reflect this.

There is a knowledge that exists beyond the separation of subject and object. This form of knowledge distinguishes itself fundamentally from the conventional, scientific knowledge. At least up until now. God cannot be proven through conventional science. The term God is also not appropriate here. Perhaps we could replace the word God with Reality.

What is Reality? That is an interesting question.

I already asked myself this question as a student in the sixties, read Hegel, Feuerbach, Marx, Habermas, Buddhist and Tibetan philosophies, Kashmir Shaivism, Sufism…

What is Reality?

For me it is being the All-Nothing, the inseparable Reality.

What is Reality?

We cannot fully grasp absolute Reality yet. It continues to remain a great secret. Human beings are currently exploring what Consciousness Itself is, what life is… and there is still a lot to explore…

83. Renowned voices in quantum physics have been emphasizing that matter, as we perceive it with our senses, does not exist and that ultimately, it is emptiness that pervades everything – the Nothing – and we are a Nothing within the Nothing. This knowledge has existed for many hundreds of years. Spiritual teachers have taught exactly that, and many people have experienced it within themselves. In what relationship does the deep knowledge stand in relation to the scientific knowledge?

Yes, as far as I understand it, matter is 99.999 percent empty. That is very interesting, particularly in relation to our body, with which we human beings seem to be most identified, in the sense that we believe our "I" to be contained in it.

Now, this apparently solid body is meant to be 99.999 percent empty?

Fully allowing and experiencing this is interesting. It is by no means scary – but rather freeing, light, wonderful!

We are allowed to be empty – to be empty space. It is great that science is pointing in this direction. But this knowledge does not bring forth transcendence, which makes human beings know throughout all levels and dimensions of consciousness that they are not – or rather – that Consciousness is all that truly IS. You have to experience it.

84. Could the boom that is occurring in the field of spirituality and science also produce damage? One example would be an attitude of: "Now I've read it – everything is one, everything is connected to everything else… I've got that. Next topic." So spirituality as a popular and trendy zeitgeist topic, which we engage in as something to be consumed and soon forgotten.

Fundamentally, everything can be misused or used for the well-being of all. On a spiritual path is it possible to gain power that can be used in both directions. That this may lead to consumerism and therefore become a flatland is, of course, an existing danger.

And yet it is so incredibly precious that the spiritual dimension is accessible to so many people.

Also, it is not the case that when we read about, for example, how to swim, that we can immediately do so.

Theoretical knowledge is information that we acquire. Once we have learned how to swim, we have integrated a very complex process.

And of course it is possible to believe that we have understood All-Love, or the Power of Now, etc.

But spirituality is not primarily about an understanding, but about a way of life. In that we can assess whether we have really understood to love unconditionally as the One Heart. It requires truthfulness and sincerity – mercilessly merciful – with oneself.

Time and time again, it is about wakefulness now! And of course there are also collective trends. We are currently opening up more and more to the spiritual dimension. And that is certainly not coincidental. But in spirituality it is not about trends or popularity, etc. It is about being human –being human consciously, yes, about an awakening of the whole of humanity. It is about a leap in consciousness toward an integral consciousness, which transcends and includes the rational, mythic, magical, and archaic consciousness structures.

In short: From "I am this and that" to "I am".

Meditation and Prayer

85.   What is meditation and what is its meaning?

In the widest sense, meditation is every moment – wakeful Presence – Now!
From this perspective, everything is meditation – every moment, regardless of whether I am driving a car, doing the washing, talking to people, sitting in silence, or doing anything else. As soon as I define what meditation is, I also exclude everything that is not part of the definition.
Presence – nondual – the highest form of meditation, of prayer, beyond any separation of inner and outer, higher and lower, important and unimportant. Presence IS.
In a stricter sense, meditation is a method that helps us recognize Reality as it truly is. Through identification with "I" and "Mine", through conditioning and external sensory perceptions, we see a distorted reality. Meditation makes us realize this, makes us calm, helps us identify the shadows that cloud our Being and Becoming. It can also enable us to get a taste of the One, of THAT, which has always been. Meditation in the strict sense is, as already said, a vehicle, a method. For many people this is extraordinarily helpful. Buddhists say that it is a great fortune to be born as a human being; that it is great fortune to wish for self-realization from the depths of one's heart; and third, that it is great fortune to find a suitable path for it.

86.   How do I reach a meditative state and what do I experience in it?

Meditation leads us into Being now. Presence. Most instructions for this are very simple. In practice, we often experience it as a process that I have described in detail in my previous book Die zwölf Phasen des Gebets. Ultimately, a meditative state is a non-state: being I am That.
When I try to describe this Being-Presence within which all Becoming unites, it is endlessly still, love sings silently in radiant Consciousness that is everything and all at once, in inseparable Unity, self-revealing, self-regulating.

All forms that come and go dance in it. Awareness notices everything without distortion in all its detail, and is simultaneously transcendent.

In pure Presence there is no subject and no object. There is nobody to experience anything. That is why I cannot say that I experience a meditative state. When Presence is, there is deep peace. It is entirely still in the midst of all sounds.

We are what we are looking for: Pure Consciousness. Today many vehicles are available to us that we can use to discover what Reality is, what is Real.

87.   What can I do when thoughts keep arising?

First, it is about simply accepting that there are thoughts. When we totally embrace this fact in the moment, something changes immediately.

If we want to get rid of the thoughts, we put energy into the field of thoughts and activate it. So first accept what is, with no resistance to it, no judgment and no attachment.

Through the total acceptance we arrive fully in the moment, where the force or the light of Presence helps us. This light-force in Presence is so strong that it quiets the thoughts – perhaps even fully dissolves them. At the same time it is important to understand that we do not strive for a thought-free state in meditation. This would mean that we have a concept for what meditation should be.

We meditate without meditating, Mrs. Tweedie told us repeatedly.

No concept, no understanding, no expectation. Meditating is something dynamic, every time new. There may be times in which thoughts arise in the silence. They pass like clouds in the sky. We do not judge. Neither the one nor the other.

88.   For how long do you advise meditating daily?

Generally, a spiritual practice is a combination of daily sitting and a practice that is carried out throughout the entire day, in the midst of life. This is at least how it is conveyed in our spiritual tradition.

I cannot answer for all spiritual traditions. We meditate 30 minutes per day. If it is possible to sit for longer, this is also good. The dhyana meditation can be practiced as long as one wants.

It is never detrimental. But many people today do not have a lot of free time. Half an hour suffices. The remaining 23, 5 hours we are aware. Now – just like that.

89. Why is meditating important on a spiritual path?

Meditation as a method is simply helpful to relieve stress, to center oneself, to come into harmony with one's inner being, listen to one's inner guidance, etc. On a deeper level, the 30 minutes sitting in silence are pure joy.

It is like a mystical re-energizing that carries you through the entire day. It changes us and our perception of the world. It heals inner and outer wounds, makes us human beings who are capable of loving that which Is, more and more.

Simultaneously, it is important to understand that meditation is not a goal in itself in spirituality. The aim of every yogic path is to be present; a conscious human being in every moment and to live a life in guidance. That is, a life guided from the inner Being-Space that radiantly creates Becoming. In this way meditation is comparable to a boat that we use in order to cross the river. Once we reach the other side, we leave the boat behind.

90. What is the difference between meditation and trance?

As I do not know trance, I cannot say much about this. Meditation has to do with being present from moment to moment. Ultimately it does not even require a method, as Consciousness from moment to moment is all that is.

91. What meaning does a prayer have for you?

Presence is the highest form of prayer, Mrs. Tweedie said to us. Yes, in Presence there is no separation. The NOW is always deepest healing-radiance. I also pray for people who are sick, in need, or for entire populations that are in conflict or at war.

That is another level of prayer, but one that has been proven to be effective. We have also developed a kind of prayer that runs under the name "Golden Thread". It is a subtle contribution to the world for peace and harmony (see: www.dergoldenefaden.info).

Praying is something natural for me. As a world citizen I am awake, aware, inform myself and listen into my inner being. As everything and all is inseparably One, I am part of the Whole, and I am the Whole at the same time.

Through praying, I contribute in a particular way. Simultaneously, we support projects in the Third World, advocate openly for One World in terms of a consciousness change on the Bundesplatz in Switzerland, "birth" the Forum for Universal Cooperation, which is meant to be a sort of container for all people on Earth.

What is a prayer, what is not a prayer?

92. Which inner, and also outer, posture do you advise taking on in prayer?

When we are beginners in prayer, it is good to pause, come to our senses, observe, become aware of where we are and what is. The body posture is not so important for this. We can pray while standing, sitting, or lying.

The moment is important, the intensity and depth of the moment, out of which a prayer arises. In addition to all this advice it is also important that we are a friend to ourselves; that we treat ourselves gently and assertively. Sometimes this is easier for us, sometimes less so.

We simply stay with it, until now IS NOW.

93. Could you say something about collective prayers?

Collective prayers are powerful.

When many people worldwide simply experience sympathy during a catastrophe, for example a tsunami, this has a tremendously powerful effect.

It has been shown scientifically that as a result of this, vibrations of the entire atomic structure have changed.

If all human beings smiled together for one minute from their heart, this would have an incredibly strong effect. A smile from the heart-space is a form of prayer. Being still, feeling connectedness with the Whole is also a form of prayer.

Presence from moment to moment is the highest form of prayer. When more and more people awaken, this will fundamentally change the world.

On December 22nd, the birthing of a new consciousness is celebrated in many different places worldwide. This is happening, in part, due to an initiative of Barbara Marx Hubbard who has very specific suggestions about the way we can realize the next evolutionary step on our Earth.

Another idea is finding a day during which it becomes possible for all human beings to collectively celebrate the light in everybody. This is what the Forum for Universal Cooperation is working on. The idea of the project the Golden Thread also stems from this realization.

We need millions of people who voluntarily give three minutes of their heart-light to the World. Silence has an effect! Silence and the consciousness-light of the heart have a higher frequency. Spirituality is, in essence, a raising of frequency.

Global changes are only effective today in collective, conscious togetherness.

94. There are many beautiful, old texts of prayer. Do you believe it to be good and important to recite these texts in prayer and to keep them alive through doing so, or is a prayer for you more about using your own words?

All is possible. When a text inspires me, I use it. There was a time when Mrs. Tweedie told me to use the Lord's Prayer as it is very powerful. I did so for many years at night when I couldn't sleep, or when I prayed particularly intensely for someone.
And sometimes I use my own words. But that is a very personal matter. Whatever spurs the heart of a human being and deeply inspires them is good.

95. What is your favorite text of prayer?

That without words.

96. When people cannot pray because they don't have the courage or feel ashamed, or if they are simply not used to it, what do you recommend to them?

To just give it a go. Contemplating it for too long does not do anything. It is worth a try.

97. A lot of people pray especially when they are afraid or have a wish. What is your attitude to praying?

If I am honest, it is peculiar: When we are in need we pray.
What about the rest of the time? Where is our attention?
Where does the Unnameable Divine begin and where does it end?
We also don't appreciate it when, for example, relatives only call us up when they are in need.
That is a very childish behavior that does not have anything to do with reflective self-responsibility.

98. People have been praying for thousands of years in a variety of different ways. What do you think: Why has this practice persisted through time?

Yes, human beings have always prayed. There has always been an understanding that there must be something higher, something else that has brought this world, this universe, into existence. This is, of course, a perspective of separation: I am separate from the you, the world, and separate from THAT, which is the great mystery. Instinctively, intuitively, human beings have invoked this Mystery in many different ways.

Today this understanding is changing fundamentally: Nothing is separable, all is One. There is one Reality that always is, with all forms arising in it as modifications of that One. Rooted in witnessing consciousness, in Presence, Reality is self-radiant and everything that comes and goes becomes transparent, is recognized as reflection on the mirror.

Through this, the identification with the reflections dissolves, as it is only from that perspective that the understanding of separation is possible.

The perception eventually becomes one of the heart-mirror, which is aware of the mirror reflections and its dynamics, and simultaneously recognizes what always is, inseparably One. And so prayers will change into pure Being that expresses Becoming co-creatively: Manifesting Heaven on Earth will be the new prayer of humanity.

99. And now my final question, again by Max Frisch: How do you explain to yourself that a human being does not cry when they are dying?

It touches me deeply that a human being doesn't cry when they are dying.

That is such a very fine observation by Max Frisch, There is a deep knowing reflected in it, which is inherent to every human being.

Birth and death are transition points. When a human being dies, this life – everything that has form and name – becomes transparent.

Everything that is not present during deep sleep, as Ramana Maharshi says, is changeable, mirror reflection, ultimately without Reality, that is, illusion. Those who are dying break away from this and what remains is what has always been, is and will be. Something in the human being knows of the One Reality, in which even their body, their life, yes – the entire world arising as its modifications – resonates inseparably in Unity.

They only leave behind their dress, their body, and ARE.

Annette Kaiser

Annette was born in Zurich in 1948. She is married and the mother of two adult children. After completing her studies in economics, she worked for many years in the field of development cooperation, and became involved in women's rights. In 1982 she met Mrs. Tweedie for the first time, becoming her student for 17 years. In the late 1980's opened her Tai Ji DO-School, teaching Tai Ji and Qigong, and training as well Tai Ji teachers. In 1991 Mrs Tweedie allowed her to give the first Sufi seminars. Since 1998, she has been continuing the path of the Naqshbandiyya Mujaddidiyya lineage with the permission of Irina Tweedie, guiding individuals on the path of love. In the year 2000 she developed the "Integral practice DO".

She is particularly devoted to translineage and transcultural spirituality, which implies an open, aware state of being as the natural expression of an integral way of living, leading into universal spirituality. Annette sees the 21st Century as a call to humanity to recognise itself as a part of the Whole, and to co-create in collective wisdom.

Anette Schirmer

Born in 1965, lives and works as a coach in Berlin. Since 1999 she has been leading a training institute for systemic business coaching.

www.coaching-individual.de

Schirmer-Rusch@Coaching-Individual.de

Graditude

A deep thank you, dear Annette, for your openness and clarity in answering all my questions.

It was simply beautiful to do this project with you.

May the readers have as much pleasure with this book as I did.

A big thank you also to all those who helped.

To Alexandra Reimann and Kerstin Landau for your assistance with the text editing, and to Janne Peter for the spontaneous collaboration and the wonderful title photo.

And a particular thanks to you, dear Eleah, for your rose picture.

It is simply beautiful. My heart for you.

-Anette

CPSIA information can be obtained at www.ICGtesting.com
Printed in the USA
BVOW05s1740081214

378465BV00001B/13/P